Threats and Promises

Rosemary Norman

Rosemary Norman (signature)

11. 11. 08

First published 1991 by IRON Press
5 Marden Terrace, Cullercoats
North Shields, Tyne & Wear NE30 4PD
Tel: 091–253 1901

Typeset by Roger Booth Associates
10 Bigg Market, Newcastle upon Tyne
in Bookman Light 10 point

Printed by Peterson Printers, South Shields

Cover design by Magali Fowler
Book design by Peter Mortimer

Some of these poems have previously appeared in the
following magazines and anthologies:
IRON, *The Rialto*, *Writing Women*, and *Dancing the Tightrope*
(*Women's Press*)

ISBN 0 906228 39 5

*IRON Press books are represented and distributed by
Password Books Ltd
23 New Mount Street
Manchester M4 4DE
Tel: 061–953 4009*

supported by
NORTHERN
ARTS

The Poems

photograph by John Norman

Rosemary Norman was born in London in 1946. She began writing as a child, and won several prizes at an impressionable age.

Her work has appeared in *IRON* and many other magazines, and in the anthologies *BREAD AND ROSES* (Virago), *DANCING THE TIGHTROPE* (Women's Press), *A DIFFERENT SKY* (Edward Arnold), and in *THE GOLD OF FLESH* (Women's Press). More is forthcoming in *GRANDCHILDREN OF ALBION*. This is her first collection.

Ten years ago she joined a women's poetry writing group, and in 1990 took over as organiser of the Open Poetry Conventicle, a mixed group which combines listening and talking to an invited guest, with discussion of members' own work. She very much enjoys reading and performing.

Hammersmith Bridge

The waters of the Thames
obstruct the flow
of traffic through London.
Where can it go?
It fumes at the feet of
bridges
which are nothing, no,
but roads over the river.
Not one of them will ever
turn its face
drop me in the wrong place
and crumble into the liquid below.

Hammersmith, though,
swings down from the sky
on long loops of brazen gold.
One day
as the soft, grey
skin of the old,
bridge-bound river slides away,
Hammersmith and I
will fly
with a burst from a barrel organ
home to heaven.
That will be when I must
give up my dream
of trotting up or downstream
to Chiswick or Putney;
the kind of bridge I can trust.

War Games

I ought never
to have let him have them; who knows
what dangerous little bits and pieces
he might swallow?
Too late: a battalion of
two-inch heroes is swarming the sofa.
His hand
guides the great, grey tank,
his throat rumbles,
his milk teeth spit out bullets.
To comfort, he explains
caterpillar wheels are designed for safety
on treacherous ground.

Those villains he hid
under a rocky cushion are flushed out
and fall, to a man, over the
cliff to the hearthrug
where they drown, and are eaten by sharks.
Now, here comes a helicopter, threatening
to defoliate the Busy Lizzie.
But he keeps his best bomb
at the bottom of the box: a deterrent
that works, just like the real one.
Pink cheeks, bright eyes;
I expect
tears before bedtime.

Home

(Spring 1982)

Home was once a brick wall
round you and Mother.
Father went back and forth, and you sat
on the doorstep, waiting.
There was a row of doorsteps
that was home.

When you grew big enough for geography
home was a island
coloured pink. It was small
but important. You lived there.
And besides, everyone knew,
there were other reasons.

You were sent away to defend
school history books and daily papers,
proud and homesick
and very soon, dead.
Home now is the open mouth
where your thumb will never again come to rest.

●

Houseboat

This brick suburb is intelligent,
concerned, dislikes itself
and wants to be otherwise.
It clings to London
brown and grey as a chrysalis
full of more than mere dreams:
it knows a butterfly is possible.

It could be a rainbow of them
kissing on the wing
in a bright tree with infinite branches
and plenty of fresh fruit for the children;
but the brown houses are laden
only with mortgages and chores
and under the grey tiles
wives and husbands forget each other
and sleep off
that after-dinner butterfly.

Sad monster,
it struggles and bursts out
blinded by tears and litigation.
Its wings, brushing our eyes and faces,
populate the streets with
wives' lovers
lovers' husbands
husbands' lovers
lovers' wives
and the houses, unmoved, revert to desirable
property, close to parks and the river.

I could live safer on one of these houseboats;
or even in a brown house
if it rocked on the earth enough
to keep me awake.

●

Another Woman

Your voice on the telephone
is thin as wire.
I say hello – what else – and
can I speak to...?
I give you my name – what else?

I could tell you how
you have fattened, these last weeks
inside my skin;
fragments of you filled out with guesswork
to life size, the size of my own life.

I could tell you: you too
fought for breath before you knew it
and later
you went on throwing open your married windows
to learn to love gusts of cold.

Then in I came
whistling to keep up my courage
and yours I hoped, and instead made you shiver.
I shiver myself
most days.

But if you answered
no, that was never me, no
it doesn't feel like that to me at all;
you could talk on
while I practised listening.

Thinly, you say
he hasn't got back yet from...I'll
tell him you called.
Yes, I have to agree, thank you –
what else?

You Could Admit No Man

You could admit no man better than you
except Gunga Din, and that was only a poem.
As for women, you married my grandmother,
a frail, nervous girl, and told me your own

had warned you about mirrors. You drew the stem
of a red rosebud down through your black lapel.
"Look at yourself too often," you said, posing
for your reflection, "and when you least expect it,

Satan looks over your shoulder." And we laughed,
both of us, knowing you could do no wrong.
I loved you best at the seaside, sweet ice-cream
melting on salty fingers, looking at rude

bosoms and bums on postcards, measuring
my understanding on grown-up jokes. And then
I caught sight of myself in brute, comic tumescence
and began to avoid mirrors. I was sixteen

the January you strode out into the snow
to get a haircut, came home and died of bronchitis.
I breathed easier. I had arrived. I knew
the worst of my life was over. It wasn't even

you, in the well-cut box, slipping away
from my womanhood, discreetly into the fire.
You were drinking beer in a seaside town I visit,
where you still call me Princess, and where you are king.

For Elaine

My friend never told me
or anyone how
her fat thighs bled in winter.
Then suddenly
there they were, naked
to the cold air of the youth club LADIES;
but for pink suspenders that scoured
her white skin, moist with doing the twist,
and with false hopes.

Her nail varnish stung
the back of my throat.
This cheap stuff is useless, she said,
except to stop ladders.
She dabbed it on her stocking and at last
stood up
and pulled her skirt down.
Well, she said, leering just a little,
no-one will see that now, will they?

Going home, she gulped chips
out of their paper bag
like aspirins out of a bottle.
Anyway, she said, my mum
told me she thinks sex is over-rated.
Trouble was, your dad was
not much good
said her auntie, years later
drunk at her wedding.

The Fat Mermaid

The fat mermaid remembers
eyes like knives
as she walked step by step
the streets of the glittering city.
Like it or not, she had
a human soul
and the soles of her feet
were more tender for being large.

Young men, handsome
with greased hair,
nudged one another and whistled.
Plain girls looked for consolation
in the helplessness of her flesh.
She crossed roads
blindly, but the song of the lorries
always stopped in time.

The loch waited, waited
till she swam
like the soul into the body
of his wide and bottomless waters,
barely raising their level.
Now, light as a ripple, in rare
moments of playfulness
she waves to a photographer.

Vegetarian Agnostic

Quiet you wait in line
for your taste of
grape's blood
and your flour and water
Jesus,
the placebo
miraculous as flesh,
you eat out of his hand.

It's more than I can
stomach, yet am I
unwholesome?
Pick my bones clean
of sin,
fling them
over your shoulder
and belch me up to heaven.

After

You did not leave a note, and would not
anyway, by then, have left one for me.
Not that I had not remembered
your going, the first time, in a chaos
of birds and spring blossom.
But I was calm, and the loss of you
was already completed.

Word of your death. Another decision
made and kept to. I will outlive you
now, twice over. Date events before, between,
between, after.
Myself, I will die
only when I must: till then
I will write notes and leave them all around me
everywhere, about everything, even this.

Waiting for Easter

Thank you he says, nicely
every Christmas to fat Uncle
who flicks out
gold coins from shirt cuffs and the child's
earholes and crushes
his little fingers round them, God
bless him, ho, ho, ho.
Thick breath and whiskery knuckles
don't make him flinch.

He has a gentle Uncle, too, takes him
praying where doves are slaughtered
and sweet smoke
lifts them up, up into the almighty nostril.
There, soft hand in soft hand, he dares
consider the bony grip
of his third and last Uncle, Balthazar,
who bit the lip of a girl cousin
under the mistletoe
with his gold tooth, the old
hypocrite, and she died.

The child will stride, soon, between
tables piled high with coins
where the gateway to the temple is narrow
as a needle's eye
only Caspar, Melchior, Balthazar, Uncles
of pomp amd piety,
can grease their way through.
Then he'll skew down towers of gold, and snatch
one poor woman caught in the wrong bed
out of a waiting whirlwind of stones.
After that
what can he do but go to the bad?

War Graves

(Photographs at the Camden Arts Centre, 1983)

The lad with the camera looks up
and a cloud blots out
the distance in his own eye.
Not a hope we'll call, one by one,
on the pale Commissioners, to report dead.
There's nothing here, nothing
they can put a name to.

Poor bastards. It's raining.
How can they find us?
We are the roots and the weather, no
escape from trampling our bones.
They don't like it. They still have names
to go by when they die.
And skins riddled with nerves.

Their soldier's made of stone,
with stiff-blown hair.
He has a stone tongue that tells over
our names, surname first and then initials.
As if we were lying in alphabetical order,
present and correct
under a weight of wings.

The Face Hospital

No, I never saw
anyone go into the face hospital
in the years I spent
the other side of the road, never,
not even from behind.
I saw it one night on TV, otherwise
never would have known
at all.

Lose
part of your face from cancer,
burns or bullets, and they are able
to mould you a brow and cheek, a
nostril and lip so perfect
(fixed to a pair
of spectacles, or piece of wig)
that even the people passing the main gates
will not see you come out.

As for going in, there must be
another door at the back.

Shadows

Black on the flat wall
our two shadows
kneel apart and repeat
each touch,
intimate and precise.

No dip or twist
of muscle, no jut of bone
or soft graze of hair.
An elongated finger traces
a breast edged with light.

But we fill the room
full with one another, draw
down between our thighs
its farthest corners.
The white wall has lost us.

You are Patient

You are patient, not
like a tree: you have legs.
Oh you praise
the patience of the scarred bark.
But roots are dragged down into the upheaval
of rock or pavement, and over or under
whatever is in the way and won't budge.
Leaves scan a single, changeable
patch of sky for light.

Walking the world with
patience, you've kept company
with trees and deserts and not troubled
either one for news of the other.
Towns arrived, that rang, each with its own
chants and coins: you prayed and traded there.
And sucking still more patience
from a pipe of opium, you dreamed
only of patient dreaming
and awoke, only awake.

Your eyes open: you smile
to find me beside you.
Smile by smile, kiss by kiss,
skin by skin by warm skin and breath on breath
we draw in the remembered
long, slow smell of one another, ourselves.
Patient we hold pleasure in our mouths and bellies
till it breaks out of us, exhausted.
Patient we question and answer
question and answer.

Patience like yours
knows no end. You dream of
spaceflights
a hundred years on and forever after...
after...after...the mystery in raised voices
has been solved, resolved.
As if patience bred patience
always as it does between us, as if
voices were raised always without reason.
As if patience had never stood up and offered itself
for brutal ill-use: your patience
brings me down in flames.

Parted from me
you would be patient, walk on
and bear it with you: I would scan and scan
the same patch of sky
and dig like tree roots to bury
the wastes of my grief.

Choreography

Playing the scene in the cell
remember it's you
who receive the blows
must carry the weight of them
to the people sitting out there.

They must read astonishment
bright in your eye,
and loneliness in the loosening
of your shoulders,
your dull-faced turning away.

These are gestures they know
and will believe in
more readily than reasons.
It's your recoil
makes them acknowledge his fist.

War Crime

Over and over
you chant aloud
the names of places never
to happen again

There it is
and there it is
and there and there and
there it is they died

Over and over
you whistle us up
to charm off new ghosts
yet to be born

Till our tired
bones click together
like marionettes and dance
to the old serenade

Acid Rain

Inside any sculpted
face is a stone
the weather will carve out,

eyes, nose and lips
worn into one
bare, unnameable sense,

calm, scanning the world.
She photographs
her damaged saints and demons,

their zeal or mischief run
in dark trickles
down the cathedral wall,

squatting and bending back
to document
ruin from every angle,

her years of indignation
nothing now
but an itch along the spine.

Bogeyman

Dead in broad daylight,
he hangs on a hook behind
the door of the foreign hotel.

This show will not go on.
No sweep of oratory
waits in his slack sleeve

and in his head no dream
of bright futures. The socialist
hangs with the dead poet

and the dead poet hangs
with the German Jew, empty
as a dressing gown that shudders

hanging on a door, and swells
huge with the dread of darkness.
The bogeyman is dead,

long live the bogeyman.
Tomorrow the Nazi papers
will claim the corpse and grin.

*Ernst Toller, the German playwright and poet, was a
charismatic political campaigner. He killed himself in
exile in New York in May 1939.*

Kind Regards

Yes, we must find a space
to park the car, since the show
alas, is about to start,

and Piccadilly sets its stony
sides against our talk, sliding us
past what we might have said.

Tomorrow you fly home.
He, too, would have made no sense
of my fervent handshake, that poet

I was so helpless to praise, dead
and much of his lifetime anyhow
crazy beyond reach,

whose words splinter me now
and break unquotable,
a kaleidoscope in the throat.

Close Science

An old sheep laid down her bones for me
at the bottom of a field. Together she and I
have observed the minutiae of dissolution,
and calculated the age
of the wrinkled moon.

Let me fly there, and smile back on the sheep's
moonlit bones, bring her home gifts, samples,
bits and pieces in jars. I will discover
the depth of each wrinkle
by shinning down it.

Oh, but my own kind escapes me, although
my hand has evolved to the shape of a caress
the moon, a bone, flesh, can run freely under.
What desperate tales
I tell myself about you!

This need there is, longing for a close science.
My mother, father, only child, my friend,
my lover, I must comprehend you, hold you better,
surely, than a mere midwife,
a surgeon, or an enbalmer.

Before Absence

Beloved, one by one
your kisses empty my mouth.

I will wash away in the morning
the tang of your skin
(when the watchful hours until you go
are kissed out at last)
and in the mirror the everyday
face of the woman alone
(who has waited all night to meet me)
will give back a clean smile.

Woman of clocks and calendars, she'll pace
this way and that among her dates and visits
till the clock stops, the map of the world
is folded and set aside,
and I lay my head on your belly.

Letter to San Francisco

Mist in the mornings, hanging between
the mountains and the sea, tangled in rooftops,
looped over steps and balconies, and wooden roses
carved into the housefronts,
hides you away. And every morning arrives
eight hours too late.

You are walking the hilly streets, up
as I go down, down
as I come up. The long bridges spin you out
to the other side of the blue bay.
I miss you.

Friendly strangers pass the telephone
from hand to hand like small change
when I say I'm calling from England.

The days run on fast, and are gone.
The days are lame, and limp by, and are gone.
An airmail letter takes a week.
It doesn't matter. It never
had the right smell.

Arrival

And at a hundred
paces, your smile
goes singing down my thighs.

I turn away, light-
headed, watch and wait until
my dumb bag bobs up
on the carousel.

I don't want it, old
leftovers, crushed together.
I want both arms free.

Lumbering
to the car, I breathe
the scent of you with moist fumes
of unconditioned air.

The streets, the city lights,
the doorkey that won't, damn it,
turn the first time... I want

Bed, oh deep and
warm grave of sense,
where the body is utterly welcome.

Oedipus Travels in Time

Oedipus travels in time, away
from that old gossip the sibyl's
echoing whisper, creeping
on all fours, but it meets him again
as he stands on his own two feet.
Foolish,
he turns back, and so
catches it up at the place
where a middle-aged stranger is killed
in an accident at the junction of three roads.
The sphinx is driven to suicide, because
all she had was her riddle, and Oedipus
wins as a prize the queen he says
now, was his own mother.
He tears out his eyes, and knowing
all the answers, hobbles off on his stick.

But the child they made me take
to the windy mountain
was a little girl, a daughter
born blind.
They won't listen, but I know
for certain she died.

Re: Rowland, Deceased, 1963

This ocean contains carnivorous fish.
Of sixty-four, the one body recovered
had died from bleeding.

Between the archipelagoes
of the South Pacific
hundreds of vessels
much like the *Melanesian*, come and go.
Doctor and Mrs Rowland shop for printed
forms, and sit at home
in Worcester Park, Surrey, to make their wills.
He leaves her what he has, unless
her death precedes or coincides with his own.
She does the same.
They will travel for three years;
two, in the event.

The court accepts that crushed and compressed
wreckage, and a single
body suggest the *Melanesian*
filled and sank with no time for recriminations,
or love whispers, or songs to God,
or thought of taking to the boats.
It cannot agree on the meaning of "coincides".

Words are peeled off words, in an unbroken
ribbon of alternative last hours.
Husband and wife, thirty-one
and twenty-eight, are raised and raised again
to a lifetime of dyings –
no, in a lifetime
they could not have lived them all.
Being three years
the younger, she is awarded
a widowhood of length unknown, down
among the wide mouths, swimming with appetite;
and three thousand pounds, inherited
from him, to leave to her niece.

What is the secret beneath
their becalmed eyelids?
That there are no eyelids, and no
Doctor or Mrs Rowland.
That that is what death is.

That the compassionate sea has dispersed
all of their little leavings.

●

Reynardine Sleeping

As the forbidden door
swings open to her touch,
the light comes down slantwise.

She sees his long-boned hand
thrown back
across his brow, the wrist veiled
finely with hairs,
the watch strap, the gold ring.

The rest is half dark.
Night after night
his nakedness is a new word
she shapes, but cannot remember.
She cannot imagine his body.
Once more it shocks her.
Yet even on the telephone, his voice
is a tongue in her ear.

Between his parted lips,
that shadow
a gleam of teeth, he breathes low.
She can kiss him and not wake him.

Strawberry Wreath

Bury me under a strawberry wreath
of green heart leaves, pale flowers
cream and brandy:

      HERE SHE LIES.

Generations of stains
on sheets cry out against us: we
the astonished few, who are delivered
alive, into the possibility
of one another's arms.

These strawberries are hearts,
are nipples.

      When you bite them
      I, too, can taste their sweetness.

Love Poem

Martens wheel and scrawl
noughts on a blank sky.
The window, half open, admits
a little evening air.

Everyone says it: the tall hero,
his heart tendered
chapter by chapter to her,
concedes it at last between kisses.
And she, like a child
trying out sounds in her mouth,
repeats it, naming him
the end of the story of her life.

Everyone says it: even the rapist,
his hand clamped fast over any answer.

And the unspoken nonsense
still, for all
my dictionary lore, and though
your tongue has cleansed my mouth
of protestation,
rises in me again.

Saline

Drip, drip. The old girl's
skinny, her bones laid out
as flat as fossils
under the sweaty blanket.
Her hair's shrivelled back
from brow and eyeholes.
Her gums chew on rough breath.
Soon she'll be dead.

And it's him, in the dim
drift of mist, her old
boy, her dear, her darling
coming for her, cock first,
bless him, as ever.
She melts, runs like summer
butter. It's good, so good, oh
yes. This is heaven.

Threats and Promises

The doctor's glasses are two
round, identical clocks. Listening
to the tick-tock of his words
she feels the last
of five hundred, perhaps,
lives that were born in her, drain away.

The mouth of her womb is narrow
but unstoppable, and full
of threats and promises as the cavern
mouth of some daft priestess.
Pain twists it
but sometimes it tells the truth.

Sometimes it sings, lets in light,
floods her fingers and toes, gobbles up
the flat earth, feeds it
and sends it flying
away like a balloon, with a child
shrieking and dancing,
hanging on to the string.

The doctor doesn't understand.
She walked out
on a good husband, doesn't try
to persuade him, but simply insists.
Does she suppose, he asks, a baby
will make her a real woman?

Shaking, she holds fast
to the fact of her flesh, the here and
now of her flesh, and a recollection
of sand crusting her knees;
when she was a girl on a beach
and played close
to the edge of the breathing sea.

Welcome

An hour late, you shrug off
questions. You knew
all the time where you were

while I sat, unravelling
your life back
to unbirth, unconception.

Son of a love misplaced
then, and now
difficult to remember

I have no welcome for you.
It is you
coming home, that welcomes me.

My Life in a Kimono

Butterfly, pink and gold, in a woven sky
Still passionately black after many washings,

Balanced on gold antennae, among pink
And white, loose-curled chrysanthemum flowers

And leaves the grey and green of coming rain.
Butterfly and chrysanthemum, you are

My one and only, ever, beautiful garment.
Sleeves, as my arms enter, slender them

To a perfect grace of turning. Now, as my hand
Loops up the sash and draws me in a waist

My breasts and hips grow tall, tall as a goddess,
Tall and yet not unfriendly, about the bow.

Like a pale kiss, there is a stain of blood
Inside, I am afraid to scrub too hard,

Where once I sat, unguarded, at my mirror,
Drying my new-washed hair to a smooth shine.

Notes to "Little St Hugh of Lincoln" poems

Charges of ritual murder against Jewish communities were common all over Europe in the middle ages. Little St Hugh of Lincoln is one of the best known of the alleged victims. He was buried as a martyr in Lincoln Cathedral in August 1255. The best known accounts of the case are in Matthew Paris' chronicles for that year, and in the ballad versions of "Little Sir Hugh" or "The Jew's daughter", collected at the end of the nineteenth century by the folklorist F.J.Child.

It seems that Hugh's body was found, perhaps in a well and perhaps in or near the Jewish quarter of Lincoln, and his mother accused the Jews. Ninety were arrested and one, Copin, confessed, on the assurance of an influential canon of the cathedral, John Lexinton, that he would be treated leniently. A few days later he was executed by order of Henry III.

The prisoners were taken to the Tower of London, and eighteen more were executed for refusing trial by an all-Christian jury. Three were released for reasons which are still obscure. Among them was Rabbi Benedict ben Moses, an eminent scholar. The wedding of his daughter, Belaset, may explain why there were more Jews than usual in Lincoln at the time of Hugh's death. The remaining prisoners were released quietly in May 1256.

In 1928 the mediaeval Jews' Court was scheduled for demolition, and there was some discussion whether the well called St Hugh's well should be preserved. Harry Staples, a builder, came forward to say he had been employed to dig the well in 1910, to enhance the tourist appeal of the property.

In the thirties Hitler tried to revive interest in St Hugh and other similar "martyrs" and was rebuffed publicly by the mayor and people of Lincoln. But the stories persist. At school in North London in the nineteen-fifties, another child told me that the local Hassidic community ate Christian babies.

Body in Well

(Matthew Paris: August 1255)

Yet another case of ritual killing
is reported today in Lincoln.
Eight-year-old schoolboy, Hugh,
was late home,
says his mother, Beatrice, a widow.
Towards dark, she called
on the child's playmates, who told her
(William shuffles and sniffs
when she asks if they've seen him.
Harold starts to cry.)
that Hugh was last seen entering the house
of Jew Jacob, also known as
Copin, pictured below.
Distraught, Beatrice herself
entered the house and discovered
her son dead in the well.
He had been brutally murdered.

Tonight, the people of Lincoln
lined the streets of the city to watch
the young martyr, Saint Hugh,
laid to rest.
A full choir, carrying candles, followed
the boy's body, which, beside the wounds
that caused his death,
(William and Harold
push to the front of the crowd.
They hold hands tightly.)
is said to bear those of Our Lord,
risen from the dead.
A woman who reached out
and touched the tips of his fingers, claims
he has cured her blindness; she saw
a light, unexplained, shining about him
and smelt, perhaps, flowers.

●

"What the Christians Say is True"

(Copin: September 1255)

"Jew," says he,
"confess to murder and to blasphemy
and by my Christian truth you will go free."
His narrow finger points up at the sky.

I confess,
I took the boy, young Hugh,
in June, and in July too,
twelve hundred and fifty-five.
I starved him, yes,
and nourished him to keep him alive
till all the Jews of England had arrived.
Let me tell you how your little children die:
we steal and crucify
to mock your God, a child, once a year.
But, you must know,
young Hugh was stabbed, for every one of us a blow;
his throat that sang so sweet was slit
and the blood drained;
also we made a cut
in the boy's belly, to fetch out his gut.
Cross-shaped. You hear?

After the sacrifice we buried what remained:
the child rose up again.
Earth was too humble to receive
his body with its uncorrupted smell.
I threw it in my well –
or my cess-pit –
as you, my accuser, most truly believe.

Does he believe such evidence?
Scholar, lawyer, man of experience?
He needs a dead saint, and I choose
to stay alive, God spare my innocence.
Where is my defence?
Was the world made for Jews?

"What the Christians say," I say, "is true."
"Yes. Yes," he whispers, "that will do."

*"What the Christians say is true" was the first line of
Copin's confession, according to Matthew Paris.*

The Jew's Daughter

(Belaset: October 1255)

I am the Jew's daughter
at the window looking out,
listening to the sons of Christians
laugh on the street corner and shout
"Can I have my ball back, mister?
Taa!"
Once or twice, slyly, I've caught
them looking in: behind me a dark room.
Kick the ball to me, I'll keep it
close as a miser, till you let me
tuck my skirt up
and join in the game.

I am the Jew's daughter
older, stepped back between shadows.
I have bathed away the last
woman's blood from my thighs, guilty as murder,
but there is more and more and more within.
Already I begin to brim.

I am the Jew's daughter
welcoming guests to my wedding.
Next day, my first child is delivered
eight years old; bloody and dead in a drinking well.
He was playing, he fell:
he kicked the ball too hard the wrong way
and scrambled, not thinking of danger,
to find it.
But one of my wedding guests is tied
to the tail of a horse,
dragged through the streets and hanged.
My father and ninety more
are bound in the Tower.

I am the Jew's daughter
lighting
candles with little hope.
I have turned my back to the window.
My father stood among his books
learned, but practical.
"Be patient," he told me, "if you lie low
a while, we can be freed.
It will blow
over, the whole affair."
Yes, it will blow,
blow like a wind of seed
over the world. It will thin in the air
till death, perhaps, may seem to have become rare.
But it will wait everywhere.

Henry is Nervous

(Benedict: December 1255)

Henry is nervous: he has a plague
of darkness in the heart
where he crusades
by himself, against the Infidel.
He counts out sins in the ear of his priest
while Holy War wastes him;
and builds churches for a better tomorrow
already part spent.
His sins are whispers: usury
is a sin.
I play king's pawnbroker
who ought to have lent him wisdom,
may God forgive us.

Henry is nervous: he believed
truly, we had murdered a child.
There were lowlier debtors who smiled.
If we had all confessed
would he have believed it? Ninety
honest Jews.
Could we have borne false witness
against ourselves, and got a true judgement?
I have kept his law, always,
as I have kept my own,
may God forgive us.

Henry is nervous: the dead boy's
mother steps up and says
I had no hand in her son's crucifixion.
Poor Beatrice, mother of nothing
but rags of flesh and a painted statue
that beckons
over the bowed heads of God's
children, sick with repentance;
who paid you the money?
And shall I be made whole by a touch of
Copin's foot, where it swings
high up in the gibbet?
Henry is nervous: he changes his mind.
I am pardonned,
may God forgive us.

Woodenchild

(Hugh: May 1256)

Don't put on your
serious face
and start asking me questions.
All you'll get is my usual
dumb smile.

Digging

(*Harry Staples: June 1934*)

The well in the Jews' Court?
I dug it myself.

Nineteen-ten.
The landlord's heart
was set on a piece of history.

So I did the job.
Filled it up with a bucket.

There was a painted sign:
ADMISSION THREEPENCE.
He paid his rent, St Hugh,
though he was dead.

Believe me, Mr Hitler,
I'd dig down
to hell to get at the bastard
who'd do harm to a child.
But the Jews' Court?
I've done with digging there.

Mary

Mary, Mary, I know you
tell lies.
They flow like dry dirt
over your fingers,
sweet with infinite shapes.
You spit on the palms of your hands
and mould them
to stop up gaps in your heart.
They set
hard, like mud.

Mary, I believe
your dad was rich, and a prince
when he lived back home
in Poland;
and nobody ever doubted
his wooden leg,
or your little sister, a mongol.
But your cat, Tiger, stolen
by the Jews next door, to trim hats
for the Sabbath?

Oh, their black wings
are folded, when they settle
on street corners, beards wagging,
jabbering all in foreign.
Some people have never
seen them fly.
But you can't fool Mary,
she can hear them at night.
So scared, she is,
sometimes she thinks she's dead.

IRON Press was formed in Spring 1973, initially to publish the magazine IRON which almost two decades, and more than 1,000 writers on, survives as one of the country's most active alternative mags – a fervent purveyor of new poetry, fiction and graphics. £8.00 gets you a subscription. Try our intriguing book list too, titles which can rarely be found on the shelves of mega-stores. Fortified by a belief in good writing, as against literary competitions or marketing trivia, IRON remains defiantly a small press. Our address is on the second page of this book